Short ish Walks
Quantocks and Mendips

Robert Hesketh

Bossiney Books · Launceston

First published 2010 by
Bossiney Books Ltd, Langore, Launceston, Cornwall PL15 8LD
www.bossineybooks.com
© 2010 Robert Hesketh All rights reserved
ISBN 978-1906474-24-9

Acknowledgements

The maps are by Nick Hawken. The cover is based on a design by Heards Design Partnership. All photographs are by the author or from the publisher's own collection.

Printed in Great Britain by R Booth Ltd, Penryn, Cornwall

Introduction

At 5-8km (3-5 miles) all the circuits in this book may be walked in a morning or an afternoon, whilst the 'there and back' walks can be completed in an hour or extended if wished. The time you need depends on how fast you walk and how interested you are in what you see – and every walk has points of interest, natural, historical or both. Rising to over 300m, both the Quantocks and the Mendips provide panoramic views from their airy hilltops, several marked by ancient forts and burial mounds. All five Quantock circuits start from one of its ring of pretty red sandstone villages (Walk 6 is a ridgeway route) whilst the Mendips' fascinating limestone gorges form the basis of four walks.

The sketch maps in this book are just that – sketches. You should go equipped with the relevant Ordnance Survey Explorer map. Sheet 140 covers all the Quantock walks and sheet 141 most of the Mendip walks. Walks 7 and 8 are on Sheet 153, Walks 17 and 18 on Sheet 142, but these walks are straightforward and you probably won't need a map.

Walking these hills is safe and trouble free as long as you are prepared with good walking boots and suitable clothing. Drinking water, map and compass, plus waterproofs and an extra layer are equally essential, as well as a comfortable rucksack. Many, including me, carry a walking stick, mobile phone and food. Please lock your car and don't leave valuables in it.

Ticks are a potential nuisance, especially in hot, humid weather. Wearing long trousers and socks offers some protection against these tiny parasites, which can carry a viral infection, Lyme disease.

Please keep to the paths over enclosed farmland, use (and close) gates as appropriate and keep dogs under control, especially near sheep.

I am sure you will enjoy these walks as I have.

Robert Hesketh

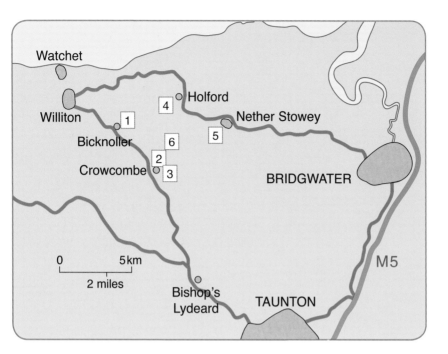

The Quantocks

'There is everything here,' wrote Dorothy Wordsworth of the Quantock hills, 'sea and woods, wild as fancy every painted.' Dorothy and her poet brother, William, spent a marvellously creative year at Alfoxton in 1797. They found inspiration with Samuel Taylor Coleridge (who lived at Nether Stowey, Walk 5) and the three explored the Quantocks with tireless enthusiasm, writing poetry on the hoof. The scenery that enchanted Dorothy remains remarkably little changed.

A whale-backed sandstone ridge rising to 384m, the Quantocks provide marvellous views over the Bristol Channel, Exmoor, the Levels and on to Dartmoor and the Brecon Beacons. They are similar to neighbouring Exmoor in their heather-covered moorland and ancient oak woods, and like Exmoor support a variety of plants and animals, including red deer and ponies.

The hills are ringed by attractive villages which retain many historic buildings. Mainly built in local red sandstone, these include several churches and inns of great character. The distant past is abundant too, with many prehistoric features including burial mounds, banks, ditches and fortified camps.

All Quantock ridge routes call for close attention to the directions because there are many paths – also used by cyclists and riders.

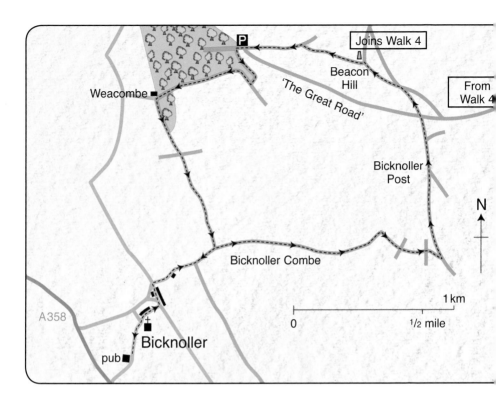

Walk 1　Bicknoller

Distance: 7km (4¹/₄ miles)
Time: 2 hours
Character: Splendid views from Beacon Hill (310m) are the highlight of this moderately demanding walk from Bicknoller, a pretty stone and thatch village with a historic church and inn.

Park considerately in CHURCH LANE. Follow Church Lane uphill. Turn left, TRENDLE LANE. Turn right into HILL LANE and follow it uphill to a gate. Continue ahead, RESTRICTED BYWAY and BICKNOLLER COMBE. Ignore side turnings and press on uphill. Fine views onto Exmoor open out behind you.

Ignore the first crosspath and continue uphill to the crest. Turn left, not onto the first grassy track but onto the second track, which is stony. Keep to the same track, passing Bicknoller Post on your right and keeping the highest point (Beacon Hill) ahead of you. Continue across 'The Great Road' – which until 1829 was the main road from Bridgwater to Watchet and Minehead. At the next crosstrack turn left and uphill to the triangulation pillar on Beacon Hill.

Bear left and downhill on a broad grassy path (see photograph above), taking a westerly course towards Porlock Bay and Exmoor. Continue to the far end of the car park.

Don't go through the gate ahead. Turn left in front of the wooden fence and down steps, signed NATIONAL TRUST. This path leads steeply downhill through trees and via more steps to Weacombe Combe.

Turn right at the T-junction and follow the path downhill, parallel to the stream. Just before you reach a row of cottages, turn left across the stream, QUANTOCK GREENWAY. Continue straight ahead at the next crosspaths.

On reaching a T-junction, turn right, downhill, and retrace your steps into Bicknoller by Hill Lane. Turn left into TRENDLE LANE then second right into Church Lane.

Bicknoller's red sandstone church is predominantly 15th century. It has many interesting features, including its 16th century carved screen and bench ends.

The thatched Bicknoller Inn has an inglenook fireplace with a bread oven, exposed ceiling beams and period photographs.

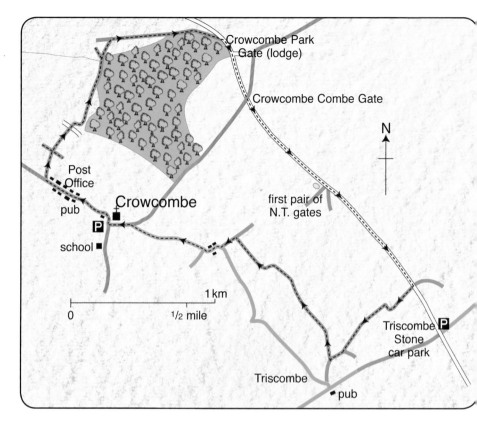

Walk 2 Crowcombe

Distance: 7.7km (4³/4 miles)
Time: 2¹/2 hours
Character: Enjoy splendid views westward over patchwork fields
to Exmoor on this fairly demanding but very rewarding walk from
Crowcombe, an attractive and interesting village.

Turn left out of Crowcombe's signed car park. Follow the lane past the church, the church house (1515) and the stone-built animal pound, and continue past the 13th century cross and the Carew Arms, a traditional inn with a log stove and hunting trophies. Some 200m beyond the post office, turn right up steps, PUBLIC FOOTPATH.

Follow the footpath steadily uphill over a series of fields and stiles, then continue uphill with a wood on your right. Finally you will emerge onto the bracken- and heather-clad hillside, where the path forks. Bear right, heading north-east, then keep right at a junction. The path circles just above the woods of Crowcombe Park, gradually heading east, then south-east before emerging at a stile onto a broader track.

Follow the edge of the estate past a gateway signed 'Crowcombe Park Gate' until you reach a lane. Cross the lane and continue ahead, TRISCOMBE STONE VIA DROVE. Follow this beautiful beech-lined drove road for 1.65 km (1 mile). Look for a pair of National Trust gates on your right – but ignore the first pair you reach! Turn right at the second pair, opposite a bridle gate.

Follow the grassy path downhill. Becoming steeper and stonier, it bends right then left to descend into Triscombe Combe. Just before you reach a wooden gate across the track, turn right at a waymark (PUBLIC FOOTPATH).

(To divert to the Blue Ball Inn at Triscombe, continue downhill through the gate and after 125 m turn left along a lane. After your visit, retrace your steps to the waymark.)

The footpath climbs steeply uphill, with a fence and hedge on the left. Then it levels out somewhat and follows the contour through trees. Continue along this path as it descends sharply into Little Quantock Combe.

Turn left at the foot of the slope and go through a bridle gate, then through a second bridle gate onto a lane. Turn right and pass Little Quantock Farm. Keep right at the first junction, then at a T-junction turn left (WILLITON TAUNTON) and continue down to the car park.

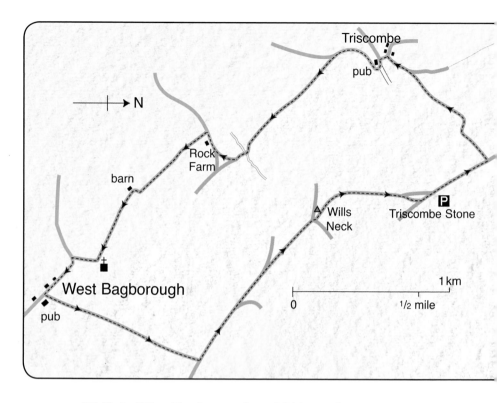

Walk 3   West Bagborough and Triscombe

Distance: 6.7km (4 miles)   Time: 2¹/₂ hours
*Character: Panoramic views from Wills Neck, the highest point on
the Quantocks, are the highlight of this beautiful but quite demanding
walk, which links the Quantock ridgeway with field paths and quiet
lanes, passing two attractive thatched inns. There is one long ascent
and one long descent.*

Park considerately at West Bagborough, on the roadside between the
church and the 'Rising Sun'. Take the tarmac track immediately to
the left of the inn. Continue ahead at a gate, RESTRICTED BYWAY. The
track climbs steadily and quite steeply for 1km.

Turn left onto the ridge track. When it divides, keep left, PUBLIC
FOOTPATH. When it divides again, 200m later, fork right and continue
uphill to the triangulation pillar on Wills Neck – by which time you've
climbed 200m (650ft).

Follow the path ahead, to the right of the pillar. This descends, levels
out, and descends again. When it divides, bear right and you should
arrive at a pair of gates. Beyond these is a very well-used track. Pass

8

the car park at 'Triscombe Stone' and continue ahead, CROWCOMBE COMBE GATE, along a handsome beech avenue – the same former drove road featured in Walk 2.

Go through a gate, then after 50m turn left at a pair of National Trust gates and follow the grassy path downhill. Becoming steeper and stonier, it bends right then left to descend into Triscombe Combe. Continue downhill to a lane and turn left.

At the 'Blue Ball Inn', turn left, then follow the lane right, behind the inn. Continue uphill on the lane, then bear left along a rough track, QUANTOCK GREENWAY.

When the track divides, keep right as signed. After another 450m, and just after crossing a brook, bear right downhill at a fork (unsigned) and join a tarmac lane at Rock Farm.

Just 50m beyond the farm, turn left at a kissing gate, QUANTOCK GREENWAY. This well signed path leads across fields by a series of gates and stiles to a large barn. From the barn, continue with the hedge on your left, then enter an enclosed path which leads to the churchyard. Walk through the churchyard, then turn right down a tarmac path. At the church gate, turn left, back towards the 'Rising Sun'.

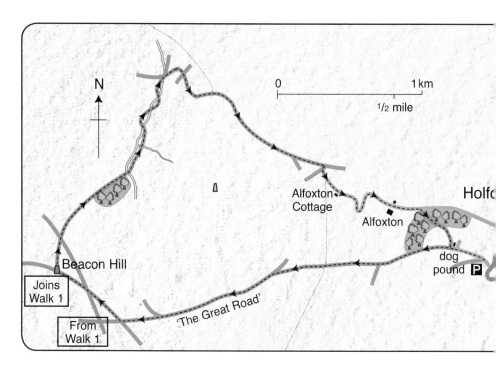

Walk 4　Holford

Distance: 7.6km (4³/₄ miles)
Time: 2¹/₄ hours
*Character: A fairly demanding walk, with a long steady ascent to
and a sharp descent from Quantock's ridge, is amply rewarded with
stunning views of the coast to east and west, plus Exmoor's stern
outline and the patchwork fields of Somerset. The Quantocks are criss-
crossed with paths and tracks so please follow the directions carefully,
and beware cyclists and horses.*

When driving from Bridgwater turn left at the Plough Inn, drive past
the pretty red sandstone church and turn right, CAR PARK.

Turn left out of the car park onto the lane, QUANTOCK GREENWAY.
(Do not take the Hodder's Combe path.) Follow the tarmac lane until
it turns right, and continue ahead, RESTRICTED BYWAY. On your right
is a curious stone structure, a dog pound bearing the St Albyn's crest
as its plaque explains.

Follow the stony track uphill, ignoring side turnings, until you
emerge from the trees and reach a junction of six paths. Continue
ahead, WEST QUANTOXHEAD STAPLE PLAIN.

Ignore side turnings until you reach a crosstracks at the crest of the ridge. Turn right and continue to another crosstracks. Continue ahead to the triangulation pillar on Beacon Hill (310m).

Turn half right and downhill. Reaching the cross track, continue ahead and downhill, SMITH'S COMBE. The path passes just to the left of trees (see photo above) then descends steeply into Smith's Combe, crossing and recrossing the brook.

At a crosspaths turn right, HOLFORD, on the QUANTOCK GREENWAY. After climbing steeply, continue ahead, HOLFORD. The path runs parallel to a wall and later a fence: ignore side turnings. At the next crosspaths turn sharp right and immediately left, uphill. The path becomes a tarmac track and leads past Alfoxton Cottage, then by steep curves to Alfoxton.

Alfoxton House was where William and Dorothy Wordsworth stayed while in the Quantocks, and where she wrote her *Alfoxden Journals*.

Continue ahead to the second cattle grid. Turn right onto a path, marked by a post and arrow. It leads steeply uphill through trees to a stile. Cross the field ahead and leave by another stile. Follow the path downhill to the dog pound and retrace your steps to the car park.

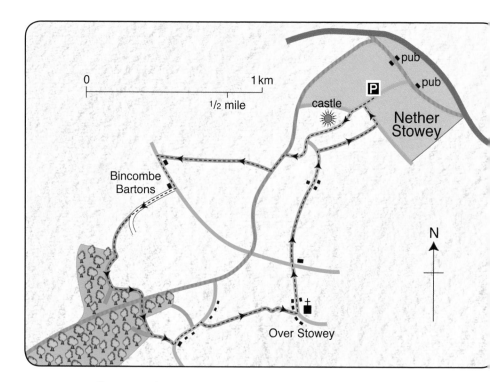

Walk 5   Nether Stowey

Distance: 5.4km (3¹/₂ miles)
Time: 1¹/₂ hours
Character: A fairly gentle (though not flat) walk by field and woodland paths and quiet lanes, with the earthworks of a castle and views over the Bristol Channel. Nether Stowey has a fine collection of historic buildings, including the poet Coleridge's sometime home.

Turn right out of the signed car park in Nether Stowey. Follow CASTLE STREET uphill for 400m. At the crest of the hill, divert right at a metal gate and cross the stile to explore Nether Stowey Castle, a motte-and-bailey structure. A helpful information board explains its history.

Retrace your steps back to the lane and turn right. Walk downhill to a T-junction. Turn left. After 120m turn right onto a path signed with a blue arrow and a quill pen – the symbol of the Coleridge Way.

Arriving at a path junction by a cottage, turn left (QUANTOCK GREENWAY). Follow the lane uphill past Bincombe Bartons and turn right onto a bridleway (blue arrow). Walk uphill on the tarmac track, then bear right away from the tarmac at a PUBLIC BRIDLEWAY sign.

Walk uphill, then when you see a bridle gate in the fence on your

right, don't go through it but bear left, up the slope to another bridle gate at the top corner of the field. This is signed PUBLIC BRIDLEWAY. Go through and walk uphill, keeping the hedgebank on your left, to a path junction. Turn left.

Continue to a lane. Cross, and follow the path ahead through trees and down to a wooden gate. A track leads from here down to another tarmac lane. Turn left along the lane and walk for 200 m past houses then cross a small stone stile on the right (PUBLIC FOOTPATH). Walk to the bottom left corner of the field, and follow the path ahead as waymarked, heading for Over Stowey and its church.

On reaching the lane by the church, turn left and follow it to a T-junction with an ash tree on an island. Take the PUBLIC FOOTPATH straight ahead. Keep straight on at a path junction by a pair of stiles and continue to a tarmac lane.

After 150 m turn right over a wooden stile opposite two bungalows. Follow the footpath across a field and to a lane. Turn left, then right at the road junction. Retrace your steps to the car park.

To explore Nether Stowey, continue past the car park to the Cross with its clock tower (1897). Turn left up Lime Street to Coleridge's Cottage, open to the public through the National Trust. The Ancient Mariner pub opposite commemorates his most famous poem.

Walk 6   Crowcombe Park Gate

Enjoy superb views from the Quantock Ridge on this there-and-back walk, which is as long as you choose to make it.

Start from the large stony parking area on the northern side of the Crowcombe-Nether Stowey lane at ST150378. Facing north, take the left of the three tracks in front of you, which heads west.

At the edge of a large estate there's a gateway marked 'Crowcombe Park Gate'. Bear right here and follow the edge of the estate, ignoring the footpath stile on the left, and following the gentle ridge track.

You could continue as far as Bicknoller Post (3.5km each way) or even further. However, some of the best views are from the cairn on Hurley Beacon (353m), one of a series of Bronze Age burial mounds on the Quantocks. Follow the track for 600m from Crowcombe Park Gate and turn left over a stile.

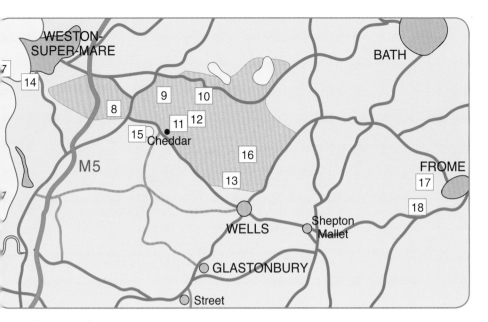

The Mendips

The Mendips, like the Quantocks, are rich in history. Ancient mine workings, prehistoric forts and a medieval castle are among the many points of interest.

The western Mendips in particular offer many splendid vistas, across the sea and over the chequerboard fields of Somerset, but the special features of these limestone hills are their deep gorges and dramatic cliffs. Two walks exploring Cheddar, Britain's largest gorge, are included here, along with circuits of Burrington Combe and Ebbor Gorge.

Both the dry springy turf of the Mendip hilltops and its deep, dry gorges developed because limestone is permeable. Rainwater (which is slightly acidic) passing through the upper layers of stone dissolves the layers beneath, especially along fissures and cracks, eventually widening them into tunnels and caverns, characterised by beautiful coloured calcite formations – the star attraction of Cheddar's caves.

During the Ice Age, water in the limestone froze, making the rock temporarily impermeable. Each summer thaw, torrents of melt water armed with scree and boulders coursed through the limestone valleys. When the Ice Age gave way to warmer conditions around 10,000 years ago the limestone thawed and became permeable again, leaving the dry gorges we see today.

15

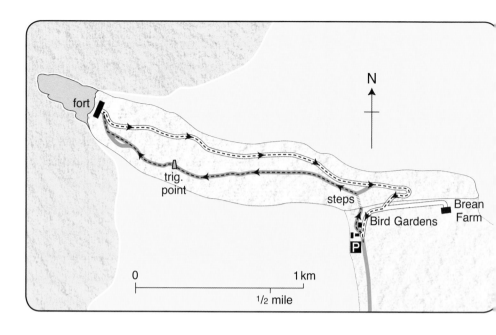

Walk 7   Brean Down

Distance: 5 km (3 miles)
Time: 1 1/2 hours
Character: Brean Down is a dramatic limestone outlier of the
Mendips, thrust like a great natural pier into the Bristol Channel.
It offers dramatic views in all directions, is a nature reserve rich in
butterflies, rare plants and birds, and has both an Iron Age and a
Victorian fort to explore. This otherwise undemanding walk involves
one short sharp climb up steps.
Please keep dogs on leads because of the steep cliffs, the grazing cattle
and goats, and nesting birds.

Take the signed public footpath at the north end of Brean Down's
National Trust car park. Keep left of the Bird Gardens and climb the
steep stepped path.

At the top of the steps turn left and follow the well-beaten path over
the turf towards the triangulation pillar (97 m above sea level) and
then on to Brean Down Fort. As you look out over the Bristol Channel
towards South Wales, you will see two islands, Steep Holm on the left
and, a little further away, Flat Holm with its lighthouse.

After exploring the fort, return by following the old military road
along the northern side of Brean Down. Continue to the further end

16

of the Down, which has the remains of what is perhaps an Iron Age fort, subsequently used by the Roman army. There are fine views of the salt marshes around the Axe estuary, with the Mendips beyond. Before these marshes formed, Brean Down was an island. As a perfect defensive site, it has been occupied at various times since the Stone Age. A Romano-British temple dating from AD 340 has also been discovered.

Follow the main path as it curves sharply right and downhill to a track junction. Turn right here, and follow the track back to the start. Be sure not to miss the free National Trust exhibition room opposite the Cove Café.

The Victorian fort, completed in 1870, was one of a series of 'Palmerston Forts' around the coast, designed to protect Britain against the resurgent power of France. It was armed with seven 7-inch muzzle-loading rifled cannons with a range of three miles. Part of the fort remains but part was dramatically blown up when Gunner Haines saw fit to fire his carbine at the gunpowder magazine in 1900. The fort was used as a café between 1905 and 1939, but was rearmed with two 6-inch guns and two searchlight batteries for the Second World War.

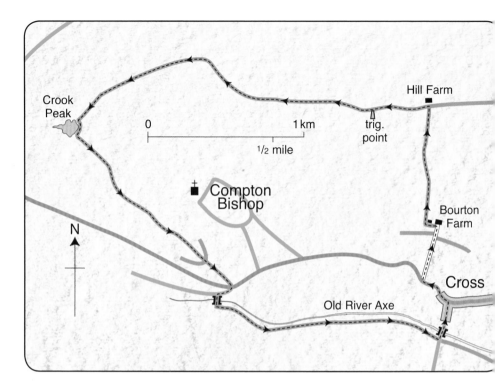

Walk 8   Cross and Crook Peak

Distance: 7.5km (4³/₄ miles)   Time: 2¹/₄ hours
A compass mght be useful when descending from Crook Peak.
Character: This superb walk by footpaths and bridleways includes two
of the best points on the 32km long Mendip Scarp – Crook Peak and
Wavering Down. Starting at sea level, the limestone scarp looks almost
mountainous, though only a modest 211m at the summit. The climb
up is rewarded with a panorama that includes Exmoor, the Quantocks,
the Bristol Channel, the Levels, Glastonbury Tor and Wales.

Park carefully on OLD COACH ROAD in Cross (ST412546). Follow the
road northwards to a T-junction. Turn left (COMPTON BISHOP) and
follow the road for 200m. Turn right into BOURTON LANE and walk
up to Bourton Farm.

Turn left in front of the farmhouse, walk past a cottage and go
through a metal gate. Turn right and walk up the field.

Take the left of two gates onto a footpath that climbs steeply. Ignore
side turnings and keep left at a fork. Walk up to Hill Farm, which lies
at the eastern end of a line of trees right at the top of the scarp.

18

At Hill Farm turn left onto the well-beaten West Mendip Way. Keep the stone wall on your right and climb to a white triangulation pillar – a relic of mapping methods before satellites and digital technology. Simply follow the main path with Crook Peak in front of you and the wall on your right for the next 2 km.

Where the wall ends, leave the West Mendip Way and follow the obvious path to the top of Crook Peak.

Walk down the southern slope of Crook Peak and follow the well-worn path in a south-easterly direction down the ridge. The village below is Compton Bishop. Ignore all side turnings and follow the ridge path above a disused quarry and down to the road.

Cross the road with care and follow the lane opposite as it passes to the right of buildings. After a short distance, turn left at a metal gate: although signed PRIVATE ROAD this is also a public footpath. Cross the Old River Axe and immediately turn left over a stile.

Follow the river bank for the next 1.5 km across fields and past a line of poplars reminiscent of France, to Old Coach Road. Turn left.

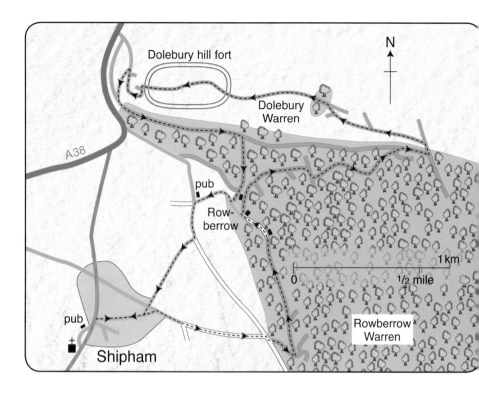

Walk 9   Shipham and Dolebury

Distance: 8.5 km (5¹/₄ miles)
Time: 2¹/₂ hours
Character: Much of this walk is through mixed woodland, but the highlight is the superb panoramic view from Dolebury hillfort. Its massive ramparts and associated field system date at least to the Iron Age. They enclose a medieval rabbit warren, where rabbits were bred for meat and fur. The walk involves one long gentle ascent and one short, sharp descent.

Park considerately in or near Shipham's main square. From the war memorial, facing away from the main road, follow HOLLOW ROAD gently uphill for 300 m. Fork right into BARN POOL. At the grassy triangle ahead, turn right along a lane signed as a cul-de-sac.

At the end of the lane, choose the middle of three paths, ROWBERROW WARREN. Waymarked CHEDDAR WEST MENDIP WAY, it leads into woodland criss-crossed with paths, so please follow the directions carefully.

Follow the path downhill to a stream. Turn sharp left, PUBLIC BRIDLEWAY. Keep the stream on your right and ignore side turnings.

Continue past cottages to a fork. Turn right, past a metal barrier. Follow the track uphill. When it divides into two bridleways, take the one on the left, slightly downhill. (Don't take the unsigned footpath.)

Do not take the next bridleway joining from the left, but 35 m further on do turn left on another bridleway. Continue to a fork in the path, and bear slightly left, then keep a fence on your right.

Continue to a T-junction and turn left. After just 50 m, turn left over a stile into grassland. Walk gently uphill on the left of the two grassy tracks ahead. Ignore a footpath off to the right and continue over a stile, LIMESTONE LINK. Follow the LIMESTONE LINK waymarks, right at a fork then left at the next junction, through trees and then along a broad grassy track.

Cross a stile and walk up to Dolebury hillfort. Enjoy the views, which include much of the Mendips, the Severn estuary and into Wales. Continue ahead on a broad grassy path and leave the fort by a gap in the western rampart. Turn left down the stony main path, which curves down past a gate to a tarmac track.

Turn left between houses down to a lane, and turn left again along it. The lane shortly becomes a track. After 800 m turn right at a waymark, LIMESTONE LINK, and follow the path uphill to a lane.

Turn right up the lane to a junction by the 'Swan Inn'. Turn left and follow the lane (ROWBERROW LANE) to a crossroads. Continue ahead on HOLLOW ROAD to the main square.

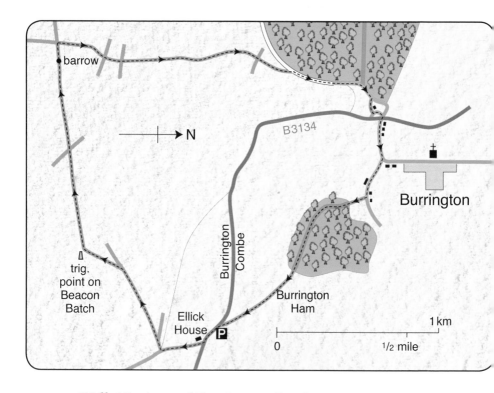

Walk 10   Around Burrington Combe

Distance: 6.6km (4 miles)
Time: 2 hours
Character: Starting from Burrington Combe, with its high limestone cliffs and feral goats, this route leads over open ground to the Mendips' highest point, Beacon Batch (325m) with tremendous views over the sea to Wales and up the estuary to the Severn Bridges, 30km away. Exmoor ponies help keep the scrub at bay, grazing the surrounding moorland and Burrington Ham.

From the parking area at the upper (eastern) end of Burrington Combe, follow the road uphill for 150m, then turn right (LIMESTONE LINK) and follow the path uphill past Ellick House.

When you reach open ground, bear right (LIMESTONE LINK). Almost immediately the path forks: keep left and climb steadily for 550m. Fork left on a stony path to reach the triangulation pillar on the summit of Beacon Batch.

Several tracks converge at the pillar. Take the sandy one on the right, heading slightly south of west. Ignore cross tracks and stay of the sandy path for 1.25km. About 100m beyond a hump in the path (a Bronze

Age barrow) turn right onto a cross track. Follow this downhill, ignoring crosstracks. To the east there is a good view of Burrington Combe.

Arriving at a T-junction by woodland, turn right down the track, and stay with it when it becomes a lane. Turn right (RUPP PUBLIC PATH) and walk steeply downhill.

Turn left at the foot of the path, then cross the B3134 with care and continue along HAM LINK. At the lane junction, continue ahead, UNSUITABLE FOR MOTORS. After 250m, turn right onto a PUBLIC BRIDLEWAY. Ignore side tracks and press on uphill, eventually emerging on the turf of Burrington Ham. Continue over the low summit of the Ham, heading towards a house, then down the far side to the parking area.

> To appreciate Burrington Combe from below, drive slowly down the Combe. Park near the western end, where climbers practise their skills and a sign proclaims the Rock of Ages. The Rev. Augustus Toplady found shelter in this split rock during a storm, and subsequently wrote the hymn 'Rock of Ages' in 1762 – long before the advent of rock music.

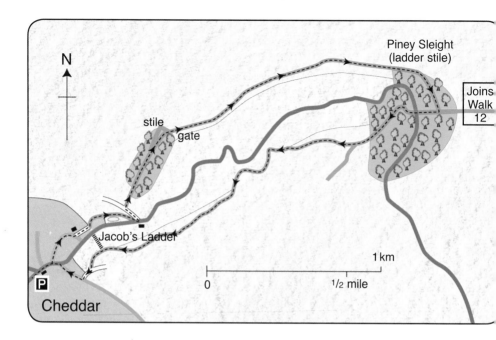

Walk 11   Cheddar Gorge

Distance: 6km (3³/₄ miles)   Time: 2 hours
Character: Cheddar Gorge is the largest gorge in Britain, over 1.6km
long and 137m deep, with towering limestone cliffs. This walk round
the upper rim provides some of Somerset's most spectacular views, but
involves two demanding ascents and descents, with uneven walking,
slippery after rain. Please keep dogs on leads and beware cliff edges.

If you're going to buy a ticket to visit the caves, buy it before the
walk as it entitles you to descend 'Jacob's Ladder'.

This walk can be combined with the much easier Walk 12. See page
26 for more details.

Turn right out of Cliff Street car park in Cheddar. Walk past the
Riverside Inn towards the gorge. Turn left just before the bridge into
The Bays and follow the lane as it swings right. Turn left past the
White Hart. Beyond the public toilets turn left, PUBLIC FOOTPATH.

On rejoining the road opposite the Tourist Information Centre, turn
immediately sharp left up a stony track. Take the first turning right,
up steps (PERMISSIVE FOOTPATH) and then climb steeply through trees.

There's more than one path, so if at the top you arrive at a stile, cross
and turn right, and after 50m you will reach a gate. But if you arrive
directly at the gate, keep right on the beaten path across the field then

24

continue gently uphill with the field wall on your right and the gorge beyond it.

Keep to the well beaten path along the rim of the gorge till it descends into Piney Sleight ('sleight' was a dialect term for a hillside sheep pasture).

Climb the ladder stile ahead of you and follow the path through trees to a track. Turn right, through a gate. Continue to the road and cross with care, taking the footpath ahead, DRAYCOTT. It climbs steeply through trees to a gate. Continue ahead, DRAYCOTT, and when the path soon divides, bear right.

You will reach a metal gate, designed to keep the feral goats in. Follow the well beaten path ahead along the southern rim of the gorge, diverting from the path to enjoy the wonderful vista.

The path descends to another goat gate. Just beyond it, if you've got a ticket turn right and descend Jacob's Ladder. At the foot, cross the road and turn left.

Otherwise, continue ahead and turn left by the viewing tower. Descend the path to a driveway and turn right. At a T-junction turn right again, then at the main street turn left over the bridge back to the car park.

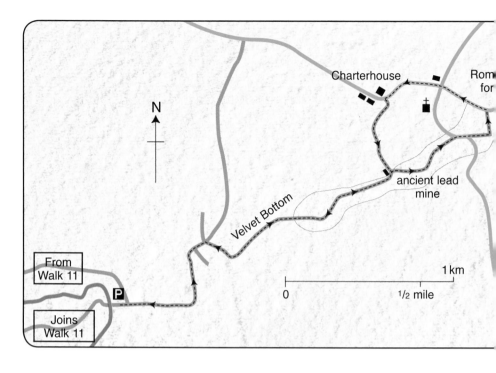

Walk 12   Charterhouse and Velvet Bottom

Distance: 6.4km (4 miles)   Time: 1 3/4 hours
Character: An easy walk – especially by comparison with Walk 11,
with which it can be combined. It traverses two nature reserves,
a limestone gorge on a miniature scale and a valley used for lead
mining from AD49, if not earlier, until 1885, but now tranquil. At
Charterhouse there are remains (not very impressive) of a Roman fort
and a Romano-British settlement.

Leave the Black Rock roadside car park (ST482545) through the
gate eastward into the Black Rock Nature Reserve. Continue into a
limestone gorge, similar to Cheddar but much smaller and without
crowds.

Turn right at the kissing gate by the Velvet Bottom Nature Reserve
sign. Follow the clear track along Velvet Bottom, past the lead mine
workings to a lane. Turn right along the lane then after 70m turn left
along the continuation of the footpath to another lane. (There is a
parking place just to the right which is an alternative starting place.)
Turn left along the lane.

To see the remains of the Roman fort, walk as far as the iron gate opposite the wind turbine, where a signboard explains that the field in front contains the fort, and another field nearby contains the Romano-British lead-mining settlement. However, the only obvious surface evidence of either occupation is humps and bumps in the ground.

Continue to the crossroads and take the lane ahead, SHIPHAM. At an S-bend, turn left (PUBLIC FOOTPATH) across a footbridge and stile. Follow the path along the valley bottom. Cross a stile, pass what at the time of writing was a boarded-up hut and turn right along the path.

Retrace your steps to the car park at Black Rock.

This walk can be combined with Walk 11 as an all-day walk. If you plan to do so, you need to know that there are no facilities of any kind at Charterhouse, nor en route, whereas Cheddar caters intensively for visitors.

You might therefore wish to start your walk from the parking area near Charterhouse.

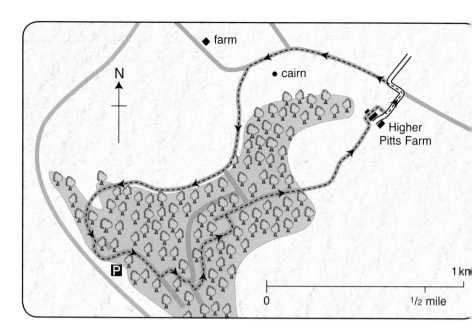

Walk 13　Around Ebbor Gorge

Distance: 4.5 km (2³/₄ miles)
Time: 1¹/₂ hours
Character: A short but demanding walk. Ebbor is a limestone gorge, accessible only on foot, similar to Cheddar Gorge and Burrington Combe but smaller. It is also a National Nature Reserve, home to a rich variety of trees, mosses and wild flowers. The clifftop viewpoint is spectacular and ample reward for the stiff ascent – but do be careful if you take children or dogs.

Park at the Hope Wood car park (ST 521484) and leave by the stone stile to the right of the display board, which outlines the geology and natural history of the gorge. Descend the steps, signed THE GORGE. After the path levels out, turn left, THE GORGE. Follow the path along the floor of the gorge to the next junction.

At this point you may wish to turn left (THE GORGE) to see the cliffs from below and thence follow the very steep path to the clifftop viewpoint. However, I recommend following an alternative route to the clifftop viewpoint as described in the next paragraph.

Turn right, then after 25 m turn left, PRIDDY. The path climbs steeply, relieved at times by steps. Continue up a second flight of steps to a T-junction of paths. Turn left at the waymark, CAUTION CLIFF AHEAD. After enjoying the vista, retrace your steps to the waymark.

Follow the now comparatively level path and continue ahead at the next sign, WEST MENDIP WAY. Cross a stile and follow the path ahead, WEST MENDIP WAY. Cross another stile, leaving the Ebbor Gorge Nature Reserve. After 200 m, when the path divides, go through a gate and keep the hedge on your left, WEST MENDIP WAY.

Head for a house (Higher Pitts Farm). Keep to the signed footpath around the left of farm buildings and join the farm driveway ahead.

Turn left, PRIDDY, then at the next junction continue ahead along Dursdon Drove. After 500 m, keep left at a fork for another 200 m. Then cross a stile on the left (PUBLIC FOOTPATH), noticing the cairn in the neighbouring field on your left. Follow the left side of the field and leave by a stone stile 50 m to the right of the field corner. Follow the footpath across another field and downhill over a stile.

At a second stile, ignore a path to the left and continue with the Ebbor Gorge woodland on your left through a series of fields.

Continue along the footpath as it descends into woodland, crosses another field then enters more woodland. At the foot of the slope, turn right across a stile and follow the path to a T-junction. Turn right, back to the car park.

Some easier and/or shorter strolls

Walk 14   Uphill

Uphill is just south of Weston-super-Mare. Use the parking area near Uphill Marina, or the parking area between Uphill Church and Uphill Marina if this is full. From the entrance to the Marina, take PUBLIC FOOTPATH UPHILL HILL AND WALBOROUGH LOCAL NATURE RESERVES (NB this path may be closed at the peak of spring tides.)

Walk past the old limekiln. Uphill church stands on the cliff above. Continue for up to 2.25km along the pleasant, well surfaced and near level footpath or, for better views of Brean Down, Weston and the coast, bear left along the broad grassy path onto Uphill Hill with its windmill tower (which has a viewing platform with explanatory plaques) and church. A steep path leads down from the church to the lane below. Turn left to return to the parking areas.

Walk 15   Axbridge

A gravelled path that circuits Cheddar Reservoir makes an easy and level walk with fine views of the Mendip scarp (see photo opposite).

Turn left out of Moorland Street car park and right across Axbridge Square, with its historic buildings, museum and church, into St Mary's Street. Walk ahead for 550m towards the edge of town. Turn right

PUBLIC FOOTPATH down an enclosed track. Only 100m ahead, at the end of the track, cross the stile on your left and walk ahead, keeping the hedge on your right. Climb a stile. Turn left. Cross another stile into woodland. Continue to a tarmac track. Simply turn right and walk up to the reservoir. Follow the path around the perimeter, returning to this point. Look out for waterfowl, especially mallard, moorhen, gulls and swans. From here, retrace your steps to the start.

Walk 16 Priddy Mineries

Park at the Forestry Commission's STOCKHILL car park, ST 548514. Leave the car park at its northern end by a 50m long joining path. Turn left and cross the road with care (PUBLIC FOOTPATH). This well beaten path leads across 'gruffy ground', which has been intensively worked for lead ore over a 2000 year period. It is now clothed in grass and reeds, though flecks of ore shine on the path. Continue for 700m to see the ponds, one with open water and one thick with reeds, both good places to watch birds.

Walk 17 Great Elm

Park carefully on the roadside near Great Elm's church, noted for its saddle-backed tower, box pews and ceiling bosses. Facing away from

the church, take the lane, JACKDAWS FROME. When the lane bends left 100 m ahead, turn right at a stile, MELLS WADBURY VALLEY. The path leads downhill through trees and then along the bank of Mells Stream (see photo above) for the next 1.75 km (1 mile).

En route are the ruins of an old iron works, where edge tools were made. It is now a breeding site for horseshoe bats. There is also a small waterfall. Turn left at the end of the riverbank path to visit Mells, a beautiful village with many historic buildings – but beware of traffic.

Walk 18 Nunney Castle and Combe

Nunney, with its moated 14th century castle (free entry), medieval George Hotel, stone built houses and church is one of the Mendips' prettiest villages. This gentle there-and-back walk crosses fields to join a bankside path by Nunney Brook.

Turn right out of the lane leading to the castle and follow the road uphill. Bear right at a small lay-by. Follow the path through trees, by-passing a little park built on a former quarry on the left. Continue to a small gate. Follow the right field edge to a second gate and the beaten path across the next field to a tree-lined embankment.

Turn right and cross the footbridge over Nunney Brook. Turn left onto the riverbank path. Reaching a track, turn left to recross the brook by a bridge. A few yards ahead, turn right at a stile PUBLIC FOOTPATH to continue along the combe by the opposite bank.